The Sainte Chapelle

The palais de la Cité

The palais de la Cité at the beginning of the 15th century, seen from the left bank, with the Sainte-Chapelle to the right showing the 13th century rose window and the canons' houses; detail of the "Month of June", a miniature in the *Très Riches Heures du duc de Berry*, by the Limbourg brothers, 1413-1416 (Chantilly, musée Condé).

A real jewel of light, universally famous for its many coloured transparency, the Sainte-Chapelle appears today as a glass and stone jewel case whose architecture and decoration the visitor admires, forgetful of the intentions of its founder, king Louis IX, the future St Louis, who had it built to house the Holy Relics of the Passion, today dispersed. This palatine reliquary chapel, whose lower part served as the parish church for the inhabitants living around the palace, became the model for all the holy chapels built by St Louis or his descendants.

A masterpiece of radiant Gothic architecture, the Sainte-Chapelle bears witness to the virtuosity of the Parisian workshops under the reign of St Louis. The sumptuousness of its decoration and the translucent beauty of its stained glass windows already amazed its founder's contemporaries who imagined themselves "introduced into one of Heaven's most beautiful rooms".

Damaged at the Revolution, the Chapelle was the object of an exemplary restoration between 1840 and 1868 in which the best artists of the different trades took part. Following the advice of Viollet-le-Duc, the architects, guided by archeological research, restored the building to its thirteenth century appearance, eliminating the later additions to its construction.

HISTORY

Paris and the kingdom of France around 1230

Louis IX was only twelve years old when he succeeded his father Louis VIII as king in 1226. The Regency was ensured by his mother, Blanche de Castille, until his coming of age and marriage with Marguerite de Provence in 1234.

Paris, which it is reckoned had a population of two hundred thousand inhabitants, was the political capital of the kingdom and the seat of

St Louis in majesty, miniature taken from the *Missel de la Sainte-Chapelle*, for the celebration of the *De sancto Ludovico rege Francorum mass*, Paris, end of the 13th century (Lyon, bibliothèque municipale).

the Chancery, Parliament and Audit Chamber; the king also had his palace there, in which the Chartes treasury housed the archives and principal royal deeds. Paris was equally the intellectual capital, with an internationally renowned University, as well as an artistic center where courtly arts were practiced–gold and silver working, tapestry making, ivory working and illumination–with building sites as prestigious as Notre-Dame.

View with horseman recreating the palais de la Cité and the Sainte-Chapelle at the beginning of the 17th century, after Jean Boisseau and Israël Silvestre, in Paris dans sa splendeur, lithograph, Paris, about 1860.

The palais de la Cité

At the heart of the Cité, on the probable site of the old residence of the Roman prefects, Philippe Auguste had built a palace that his grandson, Louis IX, altered and enlarged. It was here that he resided when he was not at Vincennes. It is very likely that besides the Sainte-Chapelle and the adjoining Chartes treasury, the future St Louis was responsible for the building of the arcade that was later to be known as the 'galerie des Merciers', (connecting the Chapelle to the king's appartments), three houses for the canons of the Chapelle, as well as the erection of the tour Bonbec and the adjoining hall, known as the 'Salle St Louis', which today no longer exists.

The Sainte-Chapelle and part of the tour Bonbec are all that remain of St Louis' palace, which served as the residence of the kings of France until 1417; it remained, however, the seat of the kingdom's judicial and financial administration.

Altered at the end of the thirteenth century by Philippe the Fair, the palace also underwent alterations during the fifteenth century and the Renaissance, before being heavily damaged by the fire of 1776 which destroyed the galerie des Merciers and led to the demolition of the Chartes treasury. Restorations undertaken during the nineteenth century and the new buildings put up mostly under the Second Empire gave the principal buildings their present day appearance.

The terms followed by an asterisk are explained in the glossary at the end of the book.

The acquisition of the relics

During the thirteenth century, the kingdom of France was rich and powerful. It maintained privileged relationships with the Middle East, and particularly with Constantinople after the town's capture by the Crusaders in 1204. In 1237, the new Franc Emperor of the East, Baudoin II de Courtenay, was faced by heavy expenses of a mainly military nature; he tried to meet these by selling the Relics of the Passion that were preserved in Byzantium and which he had already partly pledged to the Venetians. In 1239, Louis IX bought from him the Crown of Thorns worn by Christ during the Passion, for the considerable sum of one hundred and

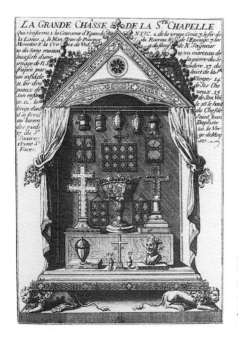

La Grande Châsse, engraving by Pierre Ransonnette in *Histoire de la Sainte-Chapelle royale du Palais*, by Sauveur-Jérôme Morand, 1790 (Paris, BNF).

The transferring* and veneration of the relics

The Crown of Thorns and the fragment of the True Cross are the most precious of all the relics bought by Louis IX from emperor Baudoin II. In 1239, wishing to greet the Crown of Thorns immediately on its arrival on his territory, the king, accompanied by his brother Robert d'Artois, bishop of Puy, the queen and Gautier Cornut, the archbishop of Sens, went to Villeneuve-l'Archevêque (today part of the Yonne), where the relic had been conveyed by the preaching friars Jacques and André de Longjumeau. The royal train escorted the Crown along the waterways as far as Paris.

From 1248 onwards, on Good Fridays, the day commemorating Christ's sacrifice, the king undertook the solemn display of the True Cross.

The most precious relics were displayed in the Sainte-Chapelle in a large reliquary gilded in silver and copper, 9 feet long, which cost one hundred thousand livres to build. Initially placed above the altar, the Large Reliquary was raised onto a platform built between 1264 and 1267.

The Large Reliquary and all the relics were melted down during the Revolution. The Crown of Thorns, deposited in 1793 in the cabinet of Antiques, was handed over to the archbishop of Paris in 1804 and is still preserved in the treasury of Notre-Dame in Paris; each Good Friday as well as the Friday before Lent, it is displayed in a reliquary designed during the nineteenth century by the architect Eugène Emmanuel Viollet-le-Duc.

Reliquary of the Crown of Thorns, illumination of the manuscript known as *Missel de la Sainte-Chapelle*, from the page of the celebration of the holy crown (Paris, BNF).

thirty five thousand livres. For the very pious Louis IX, who was the model for all the Christian kings, this was the opportunity to affirm his devotion to Christ, make his kingdom the beacon of western Christianity and support the endangered Franc Empire. Buying the relics was both a religious and a political act.

On 18 August 1239, the king deposited the Crown of Thorns with great ceremony in the former palatine chapel of St Nicholas, built in the mid twelfth century close to the palais de la Cité. Two years later, Louis IX bought a fragment of the True Cross from Baudoin II as well as other relics connected with the Passion, the Virgin and the saints; these arrived in Paris on 14 September 1241.

It is probable that from this date onwards the king thought of building a monumental reliquary to house the precious relics in a dignified manner within the palace precincts, in a similar fashion to the Christian Emperors of the East.

The idea of the Sainte-Chapelle reliquary was born. It was to have the function and form of a reliquary, as well as the sumptuous interior decoration which gives it the appearance of a monumental piece of jewelry.

The building of the Chapelle

The plan

The Sainte-Chapelle is the Gothic expression of Carolingian palatine chapels, of which the best known is the present cathedral of Aix-la-Chapelle, in Germany, built around the year 800 as an oratory for Charlemagne. In 1238, St Louis had already founded a palatine chapel adjoining the chateau of Saint-Germain-en-Laye (Yvelines), with only one storey, on which the plan of the upper chapel of the palais de la Cité is possibly based. The Sainte-Chapelle in Paris is composed of two stories of identical surface area but differing height, each with a precise function: the upper floor, on the same level as the royal appartments, housed the relics and was reserved for the king, his closest entourage and his distinguished guests; the lower floor was the palace parish, open to the king's soldiers and servants as well as to the courtiers in residence. Other double chapels were built elsewhere in France, for instance those at Laon, Reims or Meaux, for castle or episcopal use and are considered as jewels of Gothic art. The Sainte-Chapelle exceeds them all by its size and the daring of its conception. Its surface area is 56 feet wide by 118 feet long. It is 139 feet high, excluding the steeple, which places it at the forefront of Gothic cathedrals.

The building dates

The exact dates of the foundation as well as the start of building are unknown, but documents specifying dates enable us to follow the progress of the site. A bull from pope Innocent IV implies that work on the Chapelle had already begun in May 1244. In January 1246, the king founded, by an act of 'first foundation', a college of master chaplains each assisted by a priest, a clerk, a deacon and a sub-deacon, for the protection of the relics, the celebration of worship in the Chapelle, the organization of the display and the upkeep of the stained glass windows.

Seal of the Sainte-Chapelle showing the relics' platform, wax, 13th century (Paris, Archives nationales).

The Chapelle was formally consecrated on 26 April 1248 in the presence of the papal Legate, Eudes de Châteauroux, who dedicated the upper chapel to the Holy Cross, and of Pierre Berruyer, archbishop of Bourges, who consecrated the lower chapel to the Virgin. In August 1248, the king signed the second foundation act, at Aigues-Mortes, before embarking on the seventh crusade, confirming and completing the clauses of 1246.

St Louis carrying a model of the Sainte-Chapelle, miniature taken from the *Grandes Chroniques de France*, late 13th to early 14th century (Paris, bibliothèque Sainte-Geneviève).

Work must therefore have begun between the autumn of 1241 and the spring of 1244 and been completed by 26 April 1248. It took between four and six years to erect this masterpiece whose construction cost was evaluated at about forty thousand livres, according to the accounts and documents assembled for the canonization process of Louis IX.

Cross section showing the installation of different altars in the lower chapel,
the enclosure and statue of the Virgin by Germain Pilon, engraving by Pierre Ransonnette
from *Histoire de la Sainte-Chapelle royale du Palais*, by Morand, 1790 (Paris, MAP).

The furniture of the upper chapel

The chapel, no longer used today for any liturgical function, has not recovered any
of the pieces of furniture of which it was dispossessed at the Revolution.

An organ existed during the fourteenth century which was replaced first in 1493 and
then again around 1550 by an instrument, decorated with large angel musicians, that
is only known through a drawing. In 1752, the **organ** occupied the entire width of
the chapel placed infront of the first western stained glass windows. It was replaced
in 1762 by an instrument by Francois-Henri Cliquot, which can be seen today in the
Paris church of Saint-Germain-l'Auxerrois where it was transferred in 1791.

An **enclosure** situated after the second bay of the nave separated the part reserved for the king and the canons from the rest of the nave. Renovated in 1318, it was
replaced during the reign of Henri II by a sculpted wooden rood screen, against which
two altars were placed, topped by enamel plates executed in 1553 by Léonard
Limousin and today preserved in the Louvre museum.

The canons probably had no **stalls** during the thirteenth century. In 1378, the stalls
occupied the south side of the choir and during the sixteenth century they were
placed behind the rood screen. They disappeared with the Revolution.

The altar where the service was celebrated was to be found in front of the platform
with the relics. During the reign of Henri III it was decorated with marble columns
bearing bronze angels carved by the sculptor Germain Pilon.

The chief architect

No document mentions the name of the chief architect of the royal building site. An oral tradition that goes back to the sixteenth century, attributes the building of the Sainte-Chapelle and of the Chartes treasury to Pierre de Montreuil, master mason at the abbey of St Denis and chief architect of the transept at Notre-Dame in Paris.

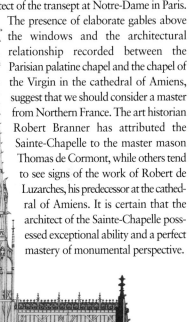

The presence of elaborate gables above the windows and the architectural relationship recorded between the Parisian palatine chapel and the chapel of the Virgin in the cathedral of Amiens, suggest that we should consider a master from Northern France. The art historian Robert Branner has attributed the Sainte-Chapelle to the master mason Thomas de Cormont, while others tend to see signs of the work of Robert de Luzarches, his predecessor at the cathedral of Amiens. It is certain that the architect of the Sainte-Chapelle possessed exceptional ability and a perfect mastery of monumental perspective.

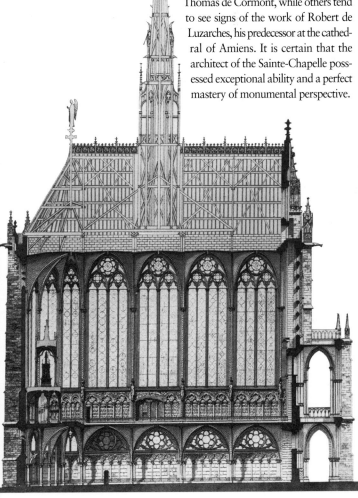

The alterations and restorations

Under the Ancien Régime

No graphic document contemporary with its building gives a complete and precise view of the Sainte-Chapelle. We owe the oldest known representation of the building to Pol de Limbourg, datable around 1413-1416: the western façade and the design of the thirteenth century rose window are clearly visible in a miniature of the *Très Riches Heures du duc de Berry*, where the palais de la Cité de Paris serves as a background to the activities of the month of June.

Later but less reliable representations, show the edifice from other angles, enabling us to follow the alterations carried out to the Chapelle and its surroundings under the Ancien Régime, before the major restoration of the nineteenth century.

The Chartes treasury, a small two storey building, built at the same time or a few years later than the Chapelle, was put up in the middle of the thirteenth century against its north side. The ground floor, which communicated with the lower chapel, contained the sacristry; the upper floor contained the revestiary. The edifice was destroyed by the fire of 1776.

In the fifteenth century, a monumental exterior staircase, built against the south wall (possibly at the request of Louis XII) led straight from the courtyard of the Sainte-Chapelle to the first floor of the porch. Destroyed by a fire in 1630, this staircase was rebuilt in 1811 before being done away with for good by the nineteenth century restorers concerned to return the building to its medieval appearance.

Documents from the seventeenth and eighteenth centuries show that a row of low structures (mainly small shops) were built against the apse.

The furniture, enriched and transformed across the centuries, was badly damaged by fires, the most devastating of which were those of 1630 and 1776. It also suffered during the Revolution when the Sainte-Chapelle was seen as the symbol of both royalty and religion.

Vue extérieure de la Sainte-Chapelle après l'incendie de 1630, drawing by Étienne Martellange (Paris, BNF).

Sortie du lit de justice de 1715, by Pierre Denis Martin, opaque watercolor, early 18th century (Paris, musée Carnavalet).

The nineteenth century restoration

From 1835 on, historians and archeologists expressed the wish to see the Sainte-Chapelle once again restored to a medieval appearance worthy of its past.

In 1840, a major archeological restoration began that was to last for more than twenty years, under the successive direction of the architects Félix Duban, Jean-Baptiste Lassus and Émile Boeswillwald who was advised by Viollet-le-Duc. This painstaking restoration, scientifically documented by the research of the archeologists Didron l'Aîné and François de Guilhermy, was an exemplary site that served as a model for subsequent restorations. The collecting together of all the original scattered fragments made it possible to study their technique and style and to

faithfully reconstruct the building's decoration. For twenty three years the Sainte-Chapelle site brought together and trained craftsmen from different corporations who subsequently worked together on other archeological sites.

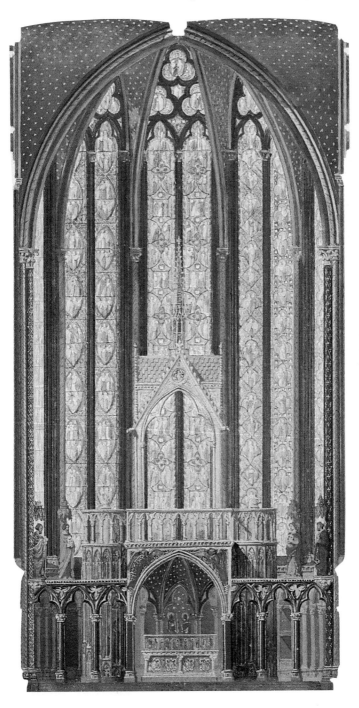

The historian Jean-Michel Leniaud has shown
to what extent this 'school site' contributed to
the revival of certain artistic activities and how
today's Chapelle is in fact closer to the work of
St Louis.

Chronology

1226-1234 Regency of Blanche de Castille.

1234 Start of the reign of Louis IX. Marriage of the king to Marguerite de Provence.

1239 Buying and transferring of the Crown of Thorns.

1241 Arrival of the True Cross and other relics.

1242-1244 Start of the building of the Sainte-Chapelle.

1246 First foundation act.

1248 Completion of the building. Formal consecration of the Sainte-Chapelle. Second foundation act. Departure of Louis IX for the seventh crusade.

1264-1267 Installation of the relics' platform.

1270 Death of Louis IX.

1297 Canonization of Louis IX.

1306 Arrival at the Chapelle's treasury of the golden reliquary containing the head of Louis IX.

Fourteenth century Building of a salient oratory against the south wall.

1383 Rebuilding of the steeple.

Fifteenth century Building of an exterior monumental staircase.

Around 1460 Replacement of the fourteenth century steeple.

1485-1498 Installation of a new western rose* window.

1630 Burning of the steeple and exterior staircase.

1690 Flooding of the lower chapel and taking down of the thirteenth century stained glass windows.

1765 Restoration of the stained glass windows in the upper chapel by Guillaume Brice, in particular the *Genesis* window.

1776 Burning of the portals and royal insignia. Secular use of the edifice. Destruction of the steeple.

1803-1837 Use of the upper chapel as an archive store.

1811 Restoration of the exterior monumental staircase.

1837 First major general restoration project.

1840-1863 Major archeological restoration of the edifice and its decoration.

1846-1855 Restoration and extension of the stained glass windows.

1853-1855 Installation of the present day steeple.

1862 The Sainte-Chapelle is classified as an historical monument; the stained glass windows are classified as an inseparable part of the building.

1918 Taking down of the stained glass in the upper chapel.

1939 Second taking down of the stained glass in the upper chapel.

1945-1947 Replacing of the stained glass in the upper chapel.

Since 1958 Restoration and upkeep of the stained glass windows by the Gaudin workshop.

1969 Restoration of the *Judith* window.

Since 1970 The research laboratory of the Monuments historiques has studied conservation problems and directed the restoration work.

1983-1984 Restoration of the paintwork of the quadrifoils in the upper chapel.

1985-1986 Restoration of the two southern bays of the apse.

1994 First national triennial partnership convention between the corporate foundation of Gaz de France and the Ministry of Culture to restore and protect the stained glass windows.

1996 Bay 2 undergoing restoration by the Gaudin workshop. Project for the installation of thermoform exterior protective glass by the Debitus workshop.

1997 Second Gaz de France triennial sponsorship convention prolonging that of 1994.

Apse and northern façade
of the Sainte-Chapelle giving
onto the cour de Mai of
the palais de justice de Paris,
seen from the boulevard
du Palais.

VISIT

The mass of the upper chapel, with its steeple dominating the administrative buildings of the palais de Justice, can be admired from the boulevard du Palais, through the railings which enclose the **cour du Mai.** A passage leads to the courtyard of the Sainte-Chapelle enabling a first view of the apse before skirting the south side of the Chapelle to enter it.

Outside architecture

The elevation

The elevation reflects the structure of the building. The massive appearance of the lower walls, whose openings are their only decoration, is opposed to the slender structure of the upper storey. The thick glacis* emphasized by a frieze of foliage, that encircles walls and buttresses, corresponds to the floor level of the upper chapel.

St Louis carrying the relic of the True Cross, 19th century statue, decorating the oratory on the south side of the chapel.

An overall feeling of balance is given by the strongly salient vertical support elements of the buttresses, which lend dynamism and rhythm to the entire building. Their unpolished, bare surfaces contrast with the fragmented ones of the stained glass windows which reflect the sun's light. Above the protruding gables that top the windows, behind the pyramidial cappings of the buttresses decorated with gargoyles, the nineteenth century restorers placed a balustrade, restored from preserved fragments of the original.

The last eastern bay of the nave is filled by the **royal oratory**, incorrectly known as the 'St Louis oratory', added during the fourteenth century between two buttresses. Only the ground floor is in good condition. All the sculpted decoration has been renovated: the great gable and the upper balustrade, decorated with monumental fleurs de lis and the large crowned L of Louis XII, are additions from the early sixteenth century; the statues of the king to the left, the bishop to the right and the Virgin and Child date from the nineteenth century.

Partial view of the superstructures with the musician angels and angels carrying the instruments of the Passion.

Statues of the apostles at the base of the spire executed by the Adolphe Geoffroy-Dechaume workshop with, under the features of St Thomas, the architect rebuilder Lassus.

Second project for the spire in the style of the 15th century, by Lassus, wash drawing, 1850 (Paris, MAP).

The steeple

The steeple that we admire today, 108 feet high, is the fifth to rise above the Chapelle since the thirteenth century. The original design remains unknown, but the second steeple, rebuilt in 1383 under the reign of Charles V, figures in a miniature in the *Très Riches Heures du duc de Berry*. The steeple that replaced it around 1460, known through several drawings and prints, was burnt in 1630; a fourth construction was in its turn destroyed in 1793. Aiming at archeological accurateness and working without any earlier documents, Lassus had the present day steeple built in the style of the fifteenth century. Begun in 1853, the work is a real technical feat executed in cedar wood by the carpenter Bellu. The sculptures that decorate the steeple as well as the apse angel were completed around 1855 in the workshop of Adolphe Geoffroy-Dechaume. The architect Lassus and the painter on glass Louis Steinheil figure amongst the apostles sculpted at the base: the first as St Thomas, recognizable by his attribution of the square which here bears the architect's name, the second as St Philip. Above the hollowed-out ornamental gables, angels carry the instruments of the Passion and give trumpet calls.

The western façade

The western façade is preceded by a strongly salient two storeyed porch, comprising a large central bay with two narrower ones on each side. The porch is overlooked by the great rose window of the upper chapel, dating from the end of the fifteenth century. At the base of the gable, a balustrade with fleurs de lis bears the initials of Charles VIII who is carried by two kneeling angels. The western mass is enclosed by the staircase turrets, whose departure is cleverly concealed in the first buttresses of the nave. Their pyramidial top is decorated with the royal crown of France and the crown of Thorns, sculpted in the fifteenth century and restored in 1845 by Geoffroy-Dechaume.

The lower chapel was reached on foot from outside, whilst the king and his guests reached the upper chapel, placed on the same level as the royal appartments, by the palace arcades.

The portal sculptures were burnt at the Revolution and the present day decoration is a restoration by Geoffroy-Dechaume that dates from the middle of the nineteenth century.

Upper part of the southern turret of the western end decorated with the crown of France and the crown of Thorns.

The lower chapel

With its height beneath the vault of only 21 feet, the chapel resembles a crypt. It is composed of a central nave 20 feet wide and very narrow side aisles seven feet wide which form the ambulatory of the apse.

The thrusts of the central vault are buttressed by elegant, small interior flying buttresses, the braces*, a particularity of the construction. The vaults of the apse are held in place by a metal structure dating from the time of construction, hidden under plaster and paint, that follows the curve of the ribs. The openings of the nave, which resemble curved pierced tympana* lined with rose windows and trifoils*, have an unusual form which Robert Branner has likened to the western bays of the side aisles in the cathedral of Amiens.

The flooding of the Seine during the winter of 1689-1690, caused important damage to the lower chapel. It particularly damaged the original paintwork and required the taking up of the floor and funerary slabs, moving of the altars and taking down of the stained glass windows. The use of the chapel as a grain store, during the Revolution, was less devastating.

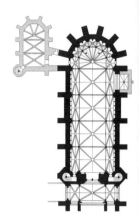

Plan of the lower chapel, by Eugène Viollet-le-Duc (*Dictionnaire raisonné de l'architecture française du XIᵉ au XVIᵉ siècle, 1854-1868*).

Porch of the lower chapel with the portal of the Virgin, engraving by Martinet, 18th century (Paris, musée Carnavalet).

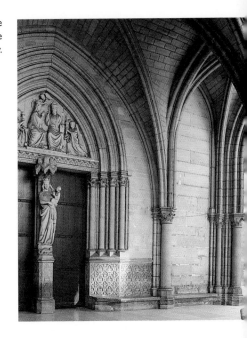

Portal of the Virgin of the lower chapel dating from the 19th century.

The sculpture

As the chapel is dedicated to Our Lady, most of the decoration of the **portal** is centered around marial iconography. The nineteenth century Virgin that decorates the pier replaced an earlier statue that was considered to be miraculous. *The Death of the Virgin*, originally sculpted on the tympana, was replaced by a *Coronation of the Virgin*. Heraldic decoration of the lower wall, where fleurs de lis alternate with the towers of Castille (the arms of Blanche de Castille Louis IX's mother), also date from the nineteenth century.

On the inside, the decoration of the one hundred and forty **capitals** of the lower chapel, executed before those of the upper chapel, is representative of the sculptural production of the Îsle de France in the first half of the thirteenth century. The artists have shown a 'generalized foliage', that is to say without reference to any precise plants, composed of trifoiled or three-pronged leaves alternating with crockets* of early Gothic foliage. The blue, red and gold paintwork added in the nineteenth century emphasizes the star pattern of the tops of the columns, where each tip corresponds with the fall of a rib of the vault.

Following double page
View of the whole of the lower chapel looking towards the choir showing the buttressing of the nave by the side struts.

The painted decoration

All the painted decoration suffered considerable deterioration from the flood of 1690. Working without old documents, the nineteenth century restorers innovated more than restored. The architectural paintwork adopted by Boeswillwald was completed in 1863.

We owe to him the painting of the vault with fleurs de lis, the heraldic motifs of fleurs de lis and Castillian towers in relief on the columns, the trompe l'œil hangings behind the blind arcades of the base and the restoration of the medallions of the twelve apostles, in which the background is enhanced by vitreous glass and the edging decorated with glass studs.

The stained glass windows

We do not know anything about the stained glass windows of the lower chapel. Taken down

Vault of the nave decorated with flowers, part of the coloured decoration designed by Émile Boeswillwald.

L'Annonciation, painting situated above the door to the former sacristy, in the lefthand side bay, restored by Steinheil after the 13th century original.

Medallion in the third northern bay: one of the twelve apostles, painted and gilded plaster.

after the flood, they were replaced shortly after 1690 by colourless stained glass windows. The present day stained glass windows, devoted to the life of the Virgin, were drawn by Steinheil during the nineteenth century. In the nave, small scenes are inscribed in a decorative grisaille*. In the apse, the two lancet* windows have full coloured glass. In the axial window we find *The Coronation of the Virgin* between *The Adoration of the Magi* to the left and, *The Presentation of Jesus in the Temple, Joseph and the Prophetess Anne* and *The Visitation* to the right. In the left lateral bay, a door led to the sacristy situated on the ground floor of the Chartes treasury. Unable to contain any stained glass, this bay was decorated in the thirteenth century by *The Annunciation* painted directly on the wall. The painting, discovered in 1849, was restored by Steinheil.

The upper chapel

The upper chapel, which is reached today by the narrow corkscrew staircases leading to the roof, amazes us by its dimensions, elevated structure, sumptuous decoration and the many coloured sparkling of the light through its stained glass windows. Built according to an extremely simple design, freeing a space 34 feet wide by 108 feet long, it is composed of a single nave with four bays, finishing in a seven-sided apse.

The walls are non-existent, replaced by surfaces of glass that appear to be of an astonishing

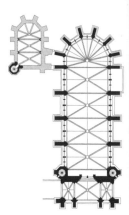

Plan of the upper chapel, by Viollet-le-Duc (*Dictionnaire raisonné de l'architecture française du XIᵉ au XVIᵉ siècle, 1854-1868*).

Portal of the Last Judgement, the upper chapel.

lightness. The glass surface, 6,458 sq. feet without the rose window, is marked by elegant stonework supports which hold up the ribbed vaulting. Their slimness is a cause for wonder, but a cluster of nine pillars cleverly disguises their real thickness. The architect has, as much as possible, transferred the supporting elements to the exterior so as to liberate a huge interior space. This architectural daring, defying the laws of balance, relies upon optical illusion and employs stratagems that demonstrate the chief architect's ability: two metal clamps*, ensure the coherence of the stonework and the glass' resistance to the wind, encircling the upper chapel halfway up the bays at the top of the lancets, where the eye mistakes them for the saddle bars* of the stained glass windows; other metal elements hidden in attics ensure that everything is held in place; the difference in height between the windows of the nave (51 feet) and those of the apse (45 feet), although

Previous double page
Stained glass windows of the north of the nave and the apse with the relics' platform.

The queen's oratory in the north wall of the third bay of the nave.

their lancets are the same size; the narrowness of the bays of the apse and the hardly visible salience of the supports enhance the extreme lightness and height of the chapel, 67 feet beneath its vault.

The sculpture

An eighteenth century description and old prints of the **portal** enabled Geoffroy-Dechaume to trace the original iconography of the sculptures. His work was also inspired by the central portal of Notre-Dame in Paris.

The pier, decorated with Christ offering benediction, supports the tympana which has a sculpted representation of the *Last Judgement*. The seated Christ, showing his wounds, is surrounded by the Virgin and St John the Baptist kneeling behind two large angels one of whom is carrying the Crown of Thorns and

Sculpted decoration of the base with angels in the spandrels.

the other the Cross (an allusion to the most remarkable of the relics preserved in the Chapelle). The *Resurrection of the Dead* figures on the lintel* with here and there *St Michael weighing the souls*. Kings and angels occupy the arch curves, at the foot of which are shown the chosen people to the left and, to the right, the damned. At the base there are bas relief sculptures of Biblical scenes, with the *Creation* to the left, and the *Story of Noah*, and that of *Cain* and *Abel* to the right.

Inside, the **continuous lower wall** with blind arches that rings the chapel can be compared with the decoration of the castral chapel of St-Germain-en-Laye. Its smooth and massive appearance contrast with the many coloured stained glass windows above from which it is separated by a frieze decorated with generalized foliage similar to that of the capitals in the lower chapel. In the corner pieces*, angels with spread wings appear from behind the clouds, some bearing crowns, others censers to glorify the martyrs painted in the quadrifoils.

Two recesses in which the royal couple sat during the services are hollowed out in the walls of the third bay of the nave; their painted decoration breaks the monotony of the lower wall. The king's oratory to the north and that of the queen to the south, are topped by richly sculpted depressed archivolts*: eight little kneeling angels cense Christ giving benediction and shown in bust form. The attention to detail and the delicate execution of this frieze sculpted

Statue of an apostle, chromolithograph from *Histoire archéologique, descriptive et graphique de la Sainte-Chapelle du Palais*, by Decloux and Doury, 1861 (Paris, MAP).

One of the six statues of the 'small apostles' in the classical style of the 1240s, stone (Paris, musée national du Moyen Âge-Thermes de Cluny).

Capital decorated with hop branches.

The apostle St Bartholomew, second southern bay.

before the middle of the thirteenth century bring to mind the precious aesthetic of Parisian ivory carvings of this period.

The thirteenth century artists who sculpted the several hundred **capitals** and consoles of the upper chapel displayed a keen sense of naturalism in characterizing each leaf. We are in the presence of second Gothic foliage, known as naturalist, with capitals decorated with thistles, leaves of oak, artemisia or buttercup, branches of hop, fig or holly, to mention just some of the plants shown, studied by the art historian Denise Jalabert. Sometimes several species are to be found on the same capital (oak, maple and may); we can also see birds pecking here and there at figs or grape seeds.

The statues of the **twelve apostles**, covered by canopies, standing against the pillars between the windows, are rightly considered as masterpieces of Gothic sculpture.

The choice of associating Christ's first disciples, true spiritual pillars of the Church, with the building's physical supports, revives the symbolic use already employed by the abbé Suger at St Denis and present in the Camera Santa d'Oviedo in Spain built at the end of the twelfth century.

The apostles of the Sainte-Chapelle, whose authors remain unknown, divide into two perfectly distinct groups. Six 'small apostles', 5 feet high, were sculpted and placed against the pillars of the apse between 1241 and 1248. Only one of them, unidentified, can today be seen in the chapel against the third southern pillar; the other statues of the group, defaced during the Revolution, are preserved in the musée national du Moyen Âge (Paris) and have been replaced in the chapel by copies made in the middle of the nineteenth century by the sculptors Adolphe Geoffroy-Dechaume, Aimé-Napoléon Perrey, Delarue and Michel Pascal. When the relics' platform was installed they were transferred to the nave because they were too small and replaced in the apse by six 'large apostles' 6 feet high, sculpted like the platform between 1264 and 1267. Three of them are still in good condition: the two at the fourth northern and southern pillars (the two St

General view of the apse with the relics' platform, during the ostentation of the Holy Crown, 15 August 1997, during the World Youth Days.

One of the two sculpted angels of the spandrels dating from the 13th century.

Jameses) and the one against the fifth northern pillar. The others have suffered the same fate as the statues of the first group. All the apostles, of whom few are identifiable, carry cruciferous discs connected with the consecration of the building. The staffs on which some of them lean where added during the nineteenth century: the paintwork of the statues was restored following traces of paintwork preserved on fragments assembled by Duban in 1841. The art historian Annette Weber has shown that the 'small apostles', belonging to a 'classical' style of around 1240, are represented barefooted like the preaching friars, unlike the 'large apostles'

Relics' platform, chromolithography from *Histoire archéologique, descriptive et graphique de la Sainte-Chapelle du Palais,* by Decloux and Doury, 1861 (Paris, MAP).

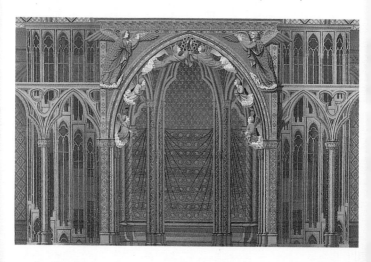

symbolizing priestly dignity, who are treated in a more precious style, associated with metalwork of around 1260.

The **relics' platform** occupied the end of the apse, where it was installed after the chapel's consecration, between 1264 and 1267. A miniature piece of architecture, it is composed of a vaulted stone kiosk with two bays, connected to the lateral walls of the apse by pierced blind arcades. At the rear, two corkscrew staircases permit access to the wooden canopy which protected the reliquary.

As the stone kiosk, northern staircase and fragments of the blind arcade escaped from the revolutionnaries' destruction, it was possible to conduct a harmonious restoration of the entire structure in 1843 with the help of miniatures and old prints. Lassus placed six angels in the central intrados bearing the instruments of the Passion that do not figure in the old documents but which harmonize with the sculpted angels of the corner stones that date from the thirteenth century.

The Martyrdom of St Sebastian, one of the forty four quadrifoils, in the first northern bay.

The painted decoration

The traces of old paintwork preciously recorded by Duban enabled him in 1842 to propose an archaelogical restoration of the painted decoration. His work consisted in fixing the parts that had been preserved, in cleaning the colours by applying hot wax and in reguilding. No trace of paint had been preserved on the lower wall and Lassus painted a false hanging in a neutral colour so as not to prejudice the vividness of the stained glass windows.

The forty four **quadrifoils**, painted in the thirteenth century directly onto the stonework of the blind arcade of the lower wall, show scenes of martyrdom standing out against gilded and chiseled backgrounds or against vitreous glass incrusted with silver or copper arabesques. The installation of the relics' platform destroyed two scenes and hid four others.

We have no precise knowledge of the restorations before Steinheil's in 1845. He made a record of thirty seven paintings; his drawings and watercolours are preserved in the musée des Monuments français in Paris. Steinheil practically completely redid the quadrifoils in the nave (though he faithfully followed the original compositions) with the exception of those in the royal oratories.

In 1968, Robert Branner was able to identify the principal martyrs through reading the old inscriptions that top them and studying Steinheil's record. In 1983, the Monuments historiques undertook the cleaning and fixing of the paint on the unrestored quadrifoils and proposed a trial restoration of two others, so as to recover their pre-1845 condition. Though the medallions of the façade and those of the choir are hardly readable, those of the nave illustrate martyrs who can often be identified. On the northern wall of the nave are to be found from west to east: the *Punishment of St Victor* attached to a wheel[36], *the*

Restoration project for the decoration of a bay, by Duban and Lassus (Paris, MAP).

Martyrdom of St Sebastian by arrows[35], three torturers torturing an unidentified saint, the *Quartering of St Hippolytus*[33] today hardly visible, the *Beheading of St John the Baptist in the presence of Salome*[32], the *Death of Thomas Becket*[31], hardly recognizable, the *Beheading of St Margaret perched on a dragon*[30], at the entrance to the king's oratory, the *Beheading of St Fermin*[29] which precedes two unrecognizable beheading scenes.

On the south wall of the nave, from east to west, the martyrdom of a saint carrying his head is recognizable[7], and also the *Punishment by iron combs inflicted on St Quentin*[8] and the *Stoning of St Etienne*[9]; after the queen's oratory, where the medallions are no longer recognizable, there are the *Beheading of St Denis*[10], *St Clement thrown into the sea*[11], *St Laurent condemned to the grill*[12], the *Flagellation of St Vincent attached to a rack*[13], an unrecognizable beheading

Painted decoration of the rear of the western façade designed and executed by Steinheil: in the tympana, Christ bestows benediction surrounded by adoring angels and, in the quadrifoils, the prophets Isaiah and Jeremiah.

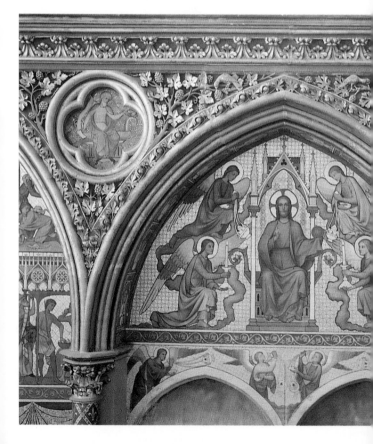

scene [14], the *Martyrdom of St Eugene carrying his head* [15], *St Blaise torn by iron combs* [16].

Although restored and in a fairly bad state of conservation, these quadrifoils are one of the few records of monumental Gothic painting. Art historians attribute the realization of the medallions, whose style is similar to that of Parisian illuminated manuscripts of around 1230-1240, to four different workshops.

The **paving** drawn by Steinheil, in hard stones incrusted with coloured putties, is decorated with animal and heraldic motifs. In the apse, four medallions allude to the rivers of Paradise.

The **rear of the façade**, originally occupied by the organ chest, received a composition by Steinheil in 1856. Above the door, between the prophets Isaiah and Jeremiah painted in medallion, the Christ presides bestowing benediction, surrounded by angels holding censers or candles. The lateral compositions illustrate biblical sacrifices: to the left: the *Immolation of the paschal lamb*, the *Blood on the houses of Hebrew*; above, *Moses and the brazen serpent*; to the right: *Abel offering the Lamb*, the *Sacrifice of Isaac by Abraham*; above, *Melchizedek offering bread and wine*.

The stained glass windows

The **upper chapel** owes its reputation to its homogeneous group of stained glass windows. The fifteen thirteenth century stained glass windows and the western rose window, replaced in the fifteenth century, give a coloured light whose intensity has always been the cause of admiration. The infinite fracturing of the colours produces a many coloured sparkling whose general tone, predominently blue and red, changes from hour to hour. These stained glass windows, composed of one thousand one hundred and thirteen figurative panels, nearly two thirds of which are original, constitute one of the jewels of the art of stained glass.

Formal programme and composition

The windows of the nave, 50 feet high and 15 feet wide, are divided into four lancets, joined together under a tympana composed of a rose window with six foils and two quadrifoils. The windows of the apse, 44 feet high and 7 feet wide, only have two lancets topped by three trifoils. The considerable homogeneity of the whole results from its overall narrative composition. The space is divided into small, well-defined scenes, held in place by saddle bars, wrought according to the various forms of the pannels*: quadrifoil, diamond, medallion, trifoil or oval*. Compositions partitioned in this manner were generally reserved for the stained glass of low windows, like those of the side aisles of the cathedral of Chartres. Here, the height of the windows and the reduced scale of the characters makes reading of a third of the scenes practically impossible by the naked eye.

The illuminated scenes are separated on an ornamental background known as the mosaic*, simple squaring or oblique lattice mainly in red and blue, concerning eight of the fifteen windows. The background is also sometimes decorated with heraldic elements, the towers of Castille and the fleurs de lis of the French crown, as is the case with seven bays and the edging of three of the stained glass windows. Curiously, Queen Marguerite of Provence, the wife of Louis IX, is hardly evoked in the building.

The narrowness of the edging does not allow the insertion of the scrolls of foliage that were customary at this period; they are reduced here to a few leaves along a shaft.

Two stained glass windows in the apse, the *Passion*, bay 0 and *Book of Daniel*, bay 2, show the variety of the forms of the panels set in the forged saddle bars.

The making of a stained glass window in the thirteenth century

The artist on glass used **sheets of glass** which he ordered from the glassworks where the glass was blown and coloured all over. The realization of a stained glass window necessitated precise and delicate manipulations; the **draft plan**, was the small scale proposition over which the artist on glass and the client reached an agreement. After approval, the artist on glass drew a charcoal **sketch*** on a table that had been whitened with chalk with the exact dimensions of each panel making up the stained glass window.

Following carefully the indications in the sketch concerning form and colour, he cut the pieces of glass with the aid of a hot **iron that had been heated by fire**.

The artist in glass always tried to take advantage of the irregularities of colour or blowing of the glass, but each change of colour demanded the cutting of a new sheet of glass.

If the design required it, the pieces of glass were painted in **grisaille***, which enabled the modification of their transparency and shading. Once painted, they were fired at 600° which fixed the grisaille.

After cooling, each piece was set in **lead rods** which were welded at their intersections. The panels thus realized were held in the bay by means of saddle bars fastened in the stone work.

Iconographical programme

Unlike the low windows of cathedrals, which generally illustrate hagiographical cycles, the windows of the Sainte-Chapelle are destined to glorify the relics of the Crown of Thorns and the True Cross.

Madame Françoise Perrot, specialist in stained glass windows, has demonstrated that the iconographical programme of the stained glass windows belongs to two separate but interdependent cycles, each corresponding to a part of the Chapelle. A first historical cycle illustrates the life of the Jewish people according to biblical accounts from *Genesis* to the *Book of Revelations*. It includes the account of the transferral of the relics, a major event during the reign of St Louis, which originated the construction of the chapel: the king of France is placed in the continuity of the kings of Israel, which makes the French royalty hiers to biblical royalty. This Old Testament narrative cycle is developed in the stained glass windows of the nave, the part of the Chapelle intended for the laity. The stained glass windows of the liturgical choir, reserved for the king and canons, illustrate the childhood and Passion of Christ surrounded by stained glass windows devoted to the St Johns: the Baptist, considered as the last of the prophets,

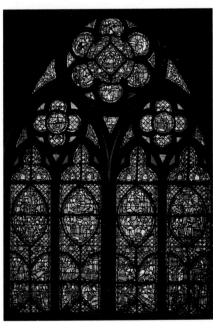

Book of Numbers, bay 9, upper half.

and the Evangelist, visionary of the Revelation. The illustration of the books of the four great prophets (Isaiah, Ezekiel, Jeremiah and Daniel) complete this prophetic cycle.

Meeting the requirements of the royal commission, the Chapelle's stained glass windows are studded with allusions to royalty: the heraldic motifs on the backgrounds or edging, the numerous representations of coronation scenes, the presence of Louis IX wearing the Christ's crown. This contemporary historical event is completed by numerous battle and idolatory scenes, which evoke the mission by which the king felt invested leaving on crusade, after the consecration of the Sainte-Chapelle.

Although we owe St Louis the overall conception of the building, there is no doubt that the king surrounded himself with theologians for the elaboration of such a complex iconographical programme. Comparisons with the moralized Bible (1230-1240) suggest that the team of scholars could have supplied the pieces of information necessary for the realization of both the illuminations and the stained glass windows.

The artists on glass

The execution of the stained glass windows required the assistance of numerous contributors who have remained anonymous. Stylistic differences would lead to suppose that the fifteen stained glass windows were executed by three different workshops, each grouping together several artists.

To the similarities of composition noted between the stained glass windows of the Sainte-Chapelle, the cathedral of Notre-Dame in Chartres and the church of Saint Germain-des-Près in Paris, are opposed stylistic differences that do not permit with any certitude the attribution of these wholes to the same workshops. Royal commissions dominated contemporary production: the glass used was of very good quality, the decoration splendid, the rapidly drawn figures executed with much verve and freedom. The striking likenesses between these stained glass windows and those of the ambulatory of the cathedral St Gervais St Protais in Soissons lead to suppose that artists from the Sainte-Chapelle site worked on the windows of the Soissons cathedral in the middle of the century. The rare panels preserved attributable to the artists in stained glass of the Sainte-Chapelle are today grouped together in the axial window.

Books of Judith and *of Job*, bay 8: *Judith at the fountains*, the workshop of the Master of Judith and Esther, 13th century.

The artists in stained glass of the Sainte-Chapelle

As is the case with most stained glass windows of the thirteenth century, none of the windows are signed in the Sainte-Chapelle. No known deal or contract enables the attribution of a stained glass window to a precise workshop.

Only stylistic analysis enabled the art historian Louis Grodecki, a specialist in stained glass windows, to distinguish three workshops who would have worked simultaneously on the stained glass executed between 1242 and 1248. So as to differentiate them, he gave each one a collective name, related to its production.

The **main workshop**, the most important and the most productive, executed the stained glass windows on the north side of the nave and apse, with the exception of the *Ezekiel* and *Daniel* windows. Its work is characterized by the suppleness of the clothing of the figures, modeled with rapidity and simplicity.

The **workshop of the Master of Ezekiel**, author of the windows of *Ezekiel*, *Daniel* and the *Kings*, employs varried compositions using figures with elongated proportions, dressed in clothing with broken and angular folds.

The **workshop of the Master of Judith and Esther**, which produced the windows of *Judith*, *Job* and *Esther*, treats the figures with a certain preciousness, giving a different expression to each. Its style evokes the illuminations of contemporary royal manuscripts.

The stained glass windows of the relics was without doubt the fruit of collaboration between the 'Main workshop' and the 'Ezekiel workshop'.

An unknown workshop that undertook the western rose window, at the end of the fifteenth century, is probably to be sought in the circle of the painter Henri de Vulcop.

The history of the restorations

Right from their installation, the upkeep of the stained glass windows came under the responsibility of the canons of the Chapelle, as is witnessed by the foundation act. Certain panels bear traces of partial restorations dating from the end of the thirteenth, fourteenth and particularly the end of the fifteenth (date of the replacement of the rose window and of several panels of the lateral windows) centuries. In the eighteenth century a pinpoint intervention was carried out on the *Genesis* window. But the stained glass windows above all suffered, between 1803 and 1837, from the use of the upper chapel as an archive store. So that shelving could be put up along the walls, the lower part of each stained glass window was walled up after removing the windows up to a height of over 6 feet. Several panels were set aside to serve as stopgaps in other windows, others, sold in antique shops, are today preserved in France and England. The major restoration of the stained glass windows was part of the nineteenth century restoration of the entire Chapelle, designed to return the building to its original appearance. The painter on glass Henri Gérente, winner of a competition that has remained famous, was unable to carry out the restoration due to premature death.

He was replaced by Antoine Lusson and, for a while, by Maréchal de Metz, with the joint authorship of Steinheil for the sketches. During this ambitious restoration, which lasted for nearly ten years (from 1846 to 1855), the different elements later than the Middle Ages or not belonging to the Chapelle were replaced (that is to say nearly a third of the stained glass windows) by panels cleverly executed in the style of the thirteenth century using the iconographical research of the archeologist Guilhermy. Thanks to these additions, which an untrained eye would be unable to recognize, the present day stained glass windows present an extraordinarily homogeneous and complete whole, close to the work commissioned by St Louis.

Reading

The narration begins at the first northern bay to the left on entering. The stained glass windows are read beginning at the bottom, from left to right, following the registers of the lower part of the lancets as far as the tympana. Only the stained glass window 14 is read following the registers from left to right then from right to left.

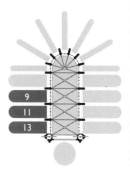

Northern side: 4 lancet stained glass windows

The Genesis[13]

91 illuminated panels in the form of medallions and half-circles: heraldic edging.

Previous double pages
Story of the relics of the Passion,
bay 14: to the right,
the Presentation of the Crown of Thorns, 13th century; to the left, the *Procession of the relics,* 19th century.

Genesis, bay 13: *Life of Joseph,* 13th century and 19th century.

This stained glass window damaged during the sixteenth century by the installation of the organ and during the eighteenth century by the construction of a wall of the palais de Justice near by, is one of the most heavily restored. Only the foils of the rose window and seven scenes from the lancets are from the thirteenth century. The recital of the Genesis begins on the lower register: the *Creation of the stars*, the *Creation of the animals*, the *Creation of Adam and Eve*, followed by the *Story of Cain*, the *Story of Abel*, the *Story of Enoch* and the *Story of Noah*. The central part of the stained glass window relates the *Life of Abraham*, the upper third the *Life of Joseph*.

The Exodus [11]

121 scenes, 92 of which are original, distributed between diamonds and cut-angled rectangles; heraldic castillian edging.

This is one of the best preserved windows. To the detailed narration of the Life of Moses, beginning with the *Finding of Moses* and the *Adoption of Moses by Pharaoh's daughter*, are mixed the principal tribulations of the Jewish people related in the book of Exodus; the *Crossing of the Red Sea*, the *Forty Days in the Desert*, the *Promulgation of the Law*.

Exodus, bay 11:
The Burning bush, 13th century.

The Book of Numbers [9]

97 illuminated panels, 70 of which are original, in the form of ovals and quarter ovals; exceptional heraldic mosaic, in which the sowing of fleurs de lis makes the stained glass windows predominantly blue and yellow.

This was the first time that the *Book of Numbers* had been illustrated in so much detail. On the lower register, several scenes of the crowning of the princes of Israel were executed from the same sketch. The cycle continues with the *Expulsion of the impure* and the account of the difficulties encountered by Moses and his people in the search for the Promised Land.

49

The Book of Joshua[7]

65 illuminated panels, 53 of which are well preserved, distributed between trifoil ovals and small quadrifoils.

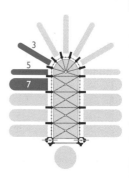

The large size of the panels make the whole of this predominantly blue stained glass window very readable. After twelve scenes devoted to Moses from the narrative of *Deuteronomy*, the *Story of Joshua*, the principal subject of the stained glass window, occupies the rest of the lancets. A large amount of space is given over to battle scenes, and the siege and taking of towns, such as Jericho. The tympana is given over to the *Story of Ruth and Boaz*.

Book of Numbers, bay 9: In the lower register, two corronation scenes executed from the same sketch, 13th century.

The 2 lancet stained glass windows in the apse

The Book of Judges[5]

64 figurative panels, only 26 of which are original. Scenes inscribed in the trifoil ovals mounted in straight saddle bars.

This rather badly preserved stained glass window was probably damaged by the eighteenth century destruction of the Chartes treasury

Book of Joshua, bay 7:
The *Fall of Jericho*, 13th century.

which stood nearby. Two panels, removed from the bay around 1850, were rediscovered in the store house of the Monuments historiques. They were restored and shown in the exhibition Vitraux de France held in Amsterdam in 1973. The iconography of this stained glass window is of great interest because it illustrates the narrative cycles of the three great judges of Israel, rarely shown. The Story of Gideon in the lower part, that of Jephthah in the middle and that of Samson in the upper third. The tympana is filled by three prophets of whom two are old.

The Book of Isaiah[3]

Left lancet: Isaiah. 24 illuminated scenes distributed between diamonds and trifoils.

Several of the scenes in this lancet, which is particularly well preserved, show great originality. Practically unknown details of the life of Isaiah are shown, such as *Isaiah holding the Christ in his arms* or *God in the wine press*. The *Martyrdom of Isaiah*, sawn in two, is one of the rare borrowings made by the artists in stained glass of the Sainte-Chapelle from the apocryphal texts.

Book of Isaiah and Jesse's Tree,
partial view of the bay 3, 13th
century and 19th century.

51

Right lancet: the Tree of Jesse. 55 regular rectangular panels held in place by straight saddle bars.

This lancet, mostly dating from the thirteenth century, is devoted to Isaiah's vision known as the Tree of Jesse, which retraces Christ's geneology. According to a median line, fourteen kings of Israel, ensure the filiation between Jesse and the Virgin, in the presence of the prophets placed at the edge. In the upper part, seven doves symbolize the gifts of the Holy Spirit. The prophets and kings, with the exception of David who is playing the viol, are not individualized. For reasons of economy and rapidity, several kings were executed from the same thirteenth century sketch; the same method was employed for the prophets. Three of them occupy the tympana.

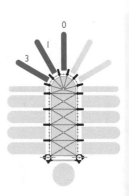

St John the Evangelist and the Childhood of Christ [1]

35 illuminated scenes in ovals.

Only eight of the stained glass windows in the left hand lancet are original, devoted to the miracles of the Evangelist and ending with the *Punishment of St John*. The right hand lancet is in better condition: after the *Virgin in the temple* and the *Annunciation*, which are modern, the old stained glass windows follow, with the *Visitation* and the *Flight into Egypt*, as well as the *Nativity*, the *Adoration of the Shepherds*, the *Announcement to the Magi* and the *Massacre of the Innocents*. The tympana bears the *Coronation of the Virgin*.

The Passion [0]

57 illuminated panels of complex form (squares, quarter circles and trifoiled protruding heraldic bosses), 42 of which are original.

The major scenes of the Passion and Christ's appearances are shown in the squares: the *Last Supper*, the *Kiss of Judas*, the *Flagellation*, the *Crowning of Thorns*, the *Crucifixion*, the *Deposition*, the *Holy Women at the Tomb*, the *Descent to Limbo*, the *Meeting at Emmaus*, the *Supper at Emmaus*. The high pictorial quality of the stained glass window has meant that it is attributed to the master of the "Main workshop". In the tympana, God the Father is placed between two angels.

The *Passion*, bay 0: The *Crowning of Thorns* and Christ's meal and the Pilgrims of *Emmaus*, "Main workshop", 13th century.

Book of Ezekiel, bay 4: The *Vision of the winged animals*, 13th century.

The Life of St John the Baptist and the Book of Daniel[2]

34 illuminated panels, 25 of which are original.

Left hand lancet: alternating diamonds and trilobes.

The story of St John the Baptist, the last prophet, evokes the main events of his life: the *Birth of St John the Baptist*, the *Baptizing of Christ*, *Herod's Banquet*, the *Imprisonment of St John the Baptist* and the *Beheading of St John the Baptist*.

Right hand lancet: succession of quadrifoils, on mosaic with castille heraldic motifs. Large fleurs de lis on the upper part.

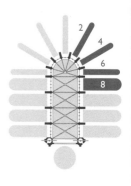

Rarely illustrated, the Book of Daniel is shown through fifteen scenes from the prophet's life, with notably, *Balthazar's Banquet*, the *Death of Balthazar* and *Daniel in the lion's den*. The tympana shows three prophets.

Book of Daniel, bay 2: Daniel in the lions' den, 13th century

The Book of Ezekiel[4]

30 illuminated quadrifoils, 16 of which are original; mosaic with castille heraldic motifs. At the top two large fleurs de lis.

Book of Ezekiel, bay 4: The Vision of the winged animals, 13th century.

The iconography of this stained glass window combines celebrated visions of the prophet Ezekiel (the *Exterminating Angels*, the *Winged Animals* or the *Restored Bones*) with lesser known parables such as the *Parable of the Green Grape*. As most of the glass is yellow, the red and yellow dominants of the mosaic give a particularly warm tonality to the entire stained glass window.

The Books of Jeremiah and of Tobit[6]

53 illuminated panels, 35 of which are original; alternation of oval and circular compartments.

Left hand lancet

The little known prophecies of Jeremiah are developed in an extraordinary manner with the *Vision of the Stove*, the *Vision of the Woman with a jackal* or the *Vision of the Ruin of Jerusalem*. Several idolatory scenes showing God's wrath are taken from the *Book of Lamentations*. The three prophets of the tympana are old. The *Birth of Jeremiah* from this bay is today preserved in the Victoria and Albert Museum in London.

Right hand lancet

The Story of Tobit, is also given particular treatment with twenty five scenes including the *Piety of Old Tobit* (the father of Tobias), the *Departure of Tobit into Captivity* where he becomes blind, the *Birth of Tobias*, the *Journey of Tobias* guided by the archangel Raphael, and the *Wedding of Tobias and Sarah*.

South side: 4 lancet stained glass windows

The Books of Judith and Job[8]

56 illuminated medallions in the lancets, 37 of which are original: heraldic mosaic sown with fleurs de lis.

The Story of Judith, the heroine of the Jewish people, fills the forty lower scenes, with notably *Holofernes' Army*, the *Siege of Bethulia*, the *Intervention of Judith*, the *Death of Holofernes*, the *Triumph of Judith* and the *Death of Judith*. For the first time in the art of stained glass, the inscriptions explaining these scenes are in French and not in Latin. The narrative of Job's sufferings is shortened to the benefit of the scenes that recount his pity and his awaiting of the divine coming. The tympana shows the *Triumph of Job*.

The Book of Esther [10]

129 illuminated panels, 100 of which are original but rather restored. Quarter circle or oval divisions connected by quadrifoil protruding heraldic bosses decorated with Castillian motifs; heraldic edging.

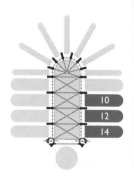

Devoting over one hundred scenes to the Story of Esther, one of the shortest accounts in the Bible, leads to repetition and going into details of the life of this Jewish heroine, who married the king of the Persians. Several scenes devoted to the *Banquets of Ahasuerus* and the queen precede the *Triumph of Mordecai* and the *Death of Haman*. The *Old Man of the Apocalypse*, in the rose of the tympana, is the only preserved panel of the thirteenth century western rose window.

The Book of Kings [12]

129 figurative panels, 98 of which are original but very restored: superposition of quadrifoil squares and indented rectangles.

The lower part of the lancets relates the Story of Samuel, followed by those of Saul and David which fill about forty panels. In the upper part, more confused scenes relate the Story of Achab, Jezebel and Joas. Strange imaginery animals decorate the heads of the lancets and are part of the original decoration. The tympana is devoted to the life of Salomon.

Book of Kings, bay 12: David presenting Goliath's head to King Saul, 19th century.

The Story of the Relics of the Passion [14]

Alternation of trifoil ovals and quadrifoils; unusual heraldic mosaic. With 27 illuminated panels out of 67, this stained glass window is the least well preserved.

The representation of the king taking part in an event of the day, at the origin of the building of the Chapelle, makes its iconography particularly interesting. The Invention* of the True Cross by St Helena, following the account of the *Golden Legend*, fills the lower half of the lancets. Better preserved, the *Acquisition of the Relics of the Passion* and the *Transferring of the Relics of the Passion* follow the text written down by Gautier Cornut, the archbishop of Sens, in 1239.

The tympana shows the adoration of the relics by the king and queen and members of the clergy and laity.

Story of the relics of the Passion, bay 14: From top to bottom, The Return of Heraclius to Jerusalem, 13th century and 19th century; Chosroes takes the relics and vases of Jerusalem, 13th century; St Helena has the True Cross placed in a chest, 19th century.

Following double page The Apocalypse, bay 15: view of the entire rose window, end of the 15th century.

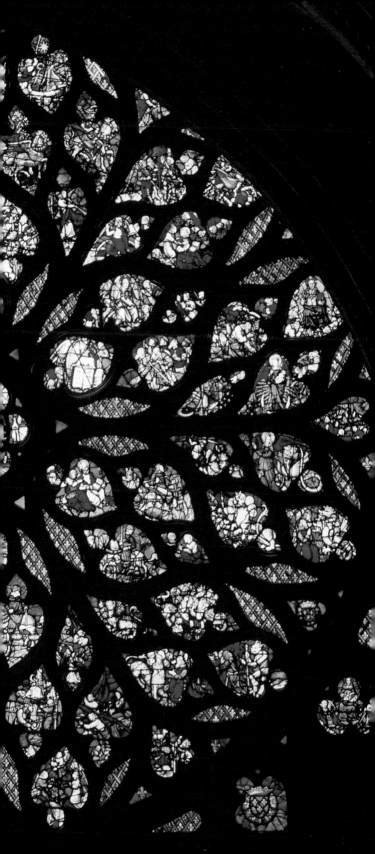

Western rose window:

The Apocalypse [15]

Rose window with a flamboyant design, 29 feet in diameter, composed of three concentric zones around a central eye. A real masterpiece of the stained glass window art of the end of the Middle Ages, composed of 89 illuminated panels, only 9 of which have been repaired.

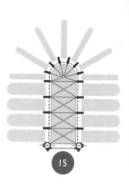

The presence of the chain of the order of St Michel which surrounds the royal arms at the top of the rose window, the technique used and the date of a royal ordonnance (1485) authorizing the canons to undertake repairs, enable the dating of the work between 1485 and 1498. The theme of the *Apocalypse* was the subject of the thirteenth century rose window of which a panel is preserved in bay 10. The iconography faithfully follows the text of the *Book of St John*. In the middle, he is prostrate at the feet of the Son of Man, surrounded by the seven lamps and seven Churches of Asia. In the first circle, are alternated the twenty four old men, the scene of the opening of the seven seals, the four symbols of the evangelists and horsemen. In the second circle, the seven angels receive the seven trumpets and announce the disasters of the end of the world, which continue in the outer circle. This latter finishes with the visions of the Woman surrounded by a halo of sun to the right, the *Combat of the King of kings* and the *Beast and the heavenly Jerusalem* to the left.

This anonymous work is of great technical quality. Close stylistically to Parisian works of the end of the fifteenth century, the stained glass window is related to illuminations of the *Petites Heures d'Anne de Bretagne*, the wife of Charles VIII, whose unknown author seems to have worked in the entourage of the painter Henri de Vulcop.

The sumptuousness of the colours of this flamboyant rose window add once again to the translucent beauty of the Chapelle which amazed St Louis' contemporaries to the point where they could imagine themselves "introduced into one of Heaven's most beautiful rooms".

The *Apocalypse*, bay 15:
The Second trumpet, the third of the sea filled with blood, end of the 15th century.

Glossary

Archivolt: Projecting molding underlining an archway.

Saddle bar: Metalic armature against which a panel of stained glass is layed.

Sketch: Life-size drawing of a work (carpet, painting, fresco or stained glass window) which serves as a model for the artist. The same sketch can be used several times.

Clamping: Metalic girdling of a building.

Crocketed capital: Sculpted capital whose decoration, imitating folded acanthus leaves, is typical of the sculpture of the first half of the thirteenth century.

Corner piece: Triangular area in the corner of an archway.

Strut: Piece of wood or metal used in architecture to avoid any separation or drawing together.

Gable: Triangular decorative top, pierced or not, topping an opening or arch.

Glacis: Sloping part of stonework.

Grisaille: Glazable colour, varying from brown to black, applied on glass to change its transparency, draw the outlines of faces or the folds of clothes, or give relief.

Decorative grisaille: Stained glass window in uncoloured glass painted in grisaille.

Lancet: Vertical division of a stained glass window.

Lintel: Horizontal cross piece above an opening.

Oculus: Circular opening in the tympana of a stained glass window or the middle of a rose window.

Panel of a stained glass window: Compartments of various shapes (trifoil, quadrifoil, rectangle, etc.) the assembling of which between two saddle bars constitutes a stained glass window.

Pinnacle: Slender, decorative architectural element.

Quadrifoil: Element in the form of a four leaved clover.

Revestiary: Gardians lodge and sacristy.

Rose window: Large circular opening in which the panels of the stained glass window are demarcated by stone mullions.

Transferring: Transfer of a saint's body from its original burial place to another place of burial.

Trifoil: Element in the form of a clover leaf.

Pier: Central pillar separating the two leaves of a portal and supporting the tympana.

Tympana: The inside area of a pediment above a portal, or the open part of a stained glass window above the lancets.

Curve of arch: Small vault over the deep embrassure of a recessed opening.

A short bibliography

Billot (Claudine), *Les Saintes-Chapelles royales et princières*, Paris, Èditions du patrimoine/CNMHS, 1998.

Branner (Robert), *The painted medallions in the Sainte-Chapelle in Paris*, Transactions of the American Philosophical Society, vol. LVIII, 2, Philadelphia, 1968.

Grodecki (Louis), *La Sainte-Chapelle*, Paris, CNMHS, 2nd edition, 1975.

Grodecki (Louis) et Brisac (Catherine), *Le Vitrail gothique au XIIIe siècle*, Paris, Vilo, 1984.

Grodecki (Louis) et Lafond (Jean), *Les Vitraux de Notre-Dame et de la Sainte-Chapelle de Paris*, "Corpus vitrearum medii aevi, France I", Paris, CNMH/CNRS, 1959.

Jalabert (Denise), *La Flore sculptée des monuments du Moyen Âge en France*, Paris, Picard, 1965.

Leniaud (Jean-Michel) et Perrot (Françoise), *La Sainte-Chapelle*, Paris, Nathan/CNMHS, 1991.

Weber (Annette), *"Les grandes et les petites statues d'apôtres de la Sainte-Chapelle de Paris"*, Bulletin monumental, v. CLV, II, 1997, p. 81-102.

The *Apocalypse*, bay 15: *St John writing*, the *Horseman holding the scales* and *Death on his horse*, end of the 15th century.